Life

The Lonely House

A Biography of Emily Dickinson

By Paul Brody

BOOKCAPS

BookCaps™ Study Guides

www.bookcaps.com

Table of Contents

About LifeCaps

LifeCaps is an imprint of BookCaps™ Study Guides. With each book, a lesser known or sometimes forgotten life is recapped. We publish a wide array of topics (from baseball and music to literature and philosophy), so check our growing catalogue regularly (**www.bookcaps.com**) to see our newest books.

Introduction

During her lifetime, Emily Dickinson did not seek out recognition or attempt to change the world around her, even in the smallest way. A private but not antisocial person, she kept her life's work, and her innermost feelings, almost entirely to herself. Her life was rich in intellectual pursuits, and she had many friends with whom she exchanged witty and brilliant letters, but she rarely left the town of her birth. From the early 1860s onward, she became essentially a recluse. After her death in 1886, it was only the good judgment of her sister Lavinia that preserved the more than 1,700 poems Dickinson had secretly produced. Her poetry was so intensely individual that it immediately captivated a national audience. More than a century later, her special genius continues to surprise readers young and old.

Chapter 1: An Unremarkable Childhood

Emily Elizabeth Dickinson was born in Amherst, Massachusetts, on December 10, 1830. She was a middle child – William Austin ("Austin") had been born the year before, while little sister Lavinia Norcross ("Vinnie") was born three years later. The Dickinson family descended from some of the earliest Puritan settlers of New England. In the 19th century, the Dickinsons of Amherst were respected, but not exactly wealthy. Her father, Edward, was a lawyer and occasionally threw himself into politics. Her mother, Emily Norcross, was a farmer's daughter from the neighboring village of Monson. In some respects, Dickinson's childhood was free of many of the hardships and heartaches so common in 19th century America. She suffered no debilitating childhood illness, and the family had money enough to ensure a good quality of life. On the other hand, the household was not without strife and dysfunction. It is likely that the unique power of Dickinson's adult poetry may have owed something to these hidden family problems, but of course no one can know for certain. Biographical information from her youth is scattered, inconsistent and often inferred from relatives' letters.

Edward Dickinson suffered from a case of too much ambition and not enough time in his day. He worked tirelessly at his own law practice while also picking up the slack of his father's business. Frequently away on business trips to Philadelphia, Washington or Boston, his wife and children saw relatively little of their breadwinner. He served multiple terms as a state legislator, and even a term as a state representative in the US Congress. Edward was determined not to repeat the mistakes of his father. Samuel Fowler Dickenson had made a series of poor business decisions, resulting in substantial monetary losses. Instead, Edward made his own, original mistakes. He was distant and unaffectionate and never formed a strong bond with either his wife or any of his three children. Dickinson remembered her father as a powerful, almost superhuman figure. When Edward was home, he often read aloud from the family Bible. His professionally polished orator's voice was more than effective at inspiring awe in his listeners.

Much less is known about Emily Norcross, but what has remained paints a picture of a reserved, secretive, perhaps even passive aggressively mean-spirited woman. Dickinson's mother grew up on a farm several miles from Amherst. Her courtship with Edward was brief and seemed to lack passion. For the two years leading up to their marriage, they only saw each other every couple of months. Compared to Edward's lengthy and business-like correspondences, Emily Norcross wrote few letters. She seemed almost to take a perverse glee in not writing back or not answering specific questions. This perverseness even extended to their impending marriage, as she was reluctant to set a date and seemed to leave everything in Edward's hands. Emily did not even visit Amherst until the wedding day had nearly arrived. Once united, life for husband and wife settled into the predictable pattern of the time, with Edward always gone and Emily typically alone at home with her thoughts and daily responsibilities.

Like her brother's the year before, Emily Dickinson's birth was not especially dangerous or painful, at least by the standards of the time. Dickinson was plump and healthy from a young age, and her mother apparently doted on her. In 1833, however, the birth of Lavinia was almost disastrous for both mother and child. Both were sickly for months, and Dickinson's mother was unable to care for her children without help. Lavinia was the last child born to the family, with Emily Norcross either unwilling or unable to tolerate another pregnancy. Fear of pain and death during childbirth was a powerful motivation for many women to delay starting a family or stop becoming pregnant after a certain number of births.

It was decided that young Emily should go to the Norcross Farm in Monson while her mother and baby sister regained their strength. Her aunt took excellent care of her, and her cousins made good playmates, but overall the experience was not a happy one. The dreaded lung disease tuberculosis, referred to at the time as consumption, had ravaged the Norcross family for generations. Dickinson's mother had only recently lost two brothers to the disease, and now one of the widows, Amanda Norcross, had fallen ill too. Emily Dickinson escaped a house of sickness only to enter a house of death. Miraculously, she herself did not contract the fatal wasting disease.

1833 was the year of another family tragedy, this one of a financial nature. Edward's father was having trouble keeping on top of the bills. Bankruptcy and foreclosure were looming possibilities. Samuel had built the all-brick Dickinson homestead (the "Brick House") in 1813, and it remained one of the most distinguished homes in Amherst. If nothing changed, he was almost certainly going to lose it and be disgraced in the community. In 1830, only a few months before Emily was born, Edward's family took up residence in the west side of the house while Samuel and his wife, Lucretia Gunn Dickinson, occupied the east side. The purpose of the arrangement was to help Samuel avoid foreclosure, but ultimately the plan failed. Samuel was forced to admit defeat; he and his wife traveled west to Cincinnati, where he took a position at Lane Theological Seminary. Emily Dickinson never saw her grandparents again.

As a child, Dickinson was not without close friends. She had a tight-knit circle of girlhood friends even before her enrollment at Amherst Academy. She would stay in contact with a few of these friends, like Abiah Wood, well into her adult life. Naturally, when she was young, her friends and playmates consisted entirely of boys and girls from the neighborhood. Her usual activities were not much different from any other child of her day and age. She enjoyed going on walks, reading, going to church and school, and learning to sing and play the piano. Apart from her absent father and emotionally stilted mother, Dickinson's childhood was ordinary in almost every way.

When Emily was nine, the family needed a place of their own, away from the awkward memories of the Brick House on Main Street. Edward was doing well in the world, and he saw no reason for his wife and children to stay on as renters in a home that once belonged to them. His success in politics and law demanded more space for the entertainment of guests and associates, and the family needed room to grow. Edward purchased a large frame house on Pleasant Street, only a short walk from the former Dickinson homestead on Main Street. Dickinson almost immediately formed a strong attachment to the place, and especially her own room.

Oddly enough, the Pleasant Street house was adjacent to the town's only cemetery. Dickinson could easily have watched every funeral procession and burial held in Amherst. Biographers have wondered whether this fact might have played a role in the development of her sometimes-morbid imagination.

Chapter 2: Education and Literary Influence

Emily Dickinson's father, Edward Dickinson, was ahead of his time in one important sense: He believed that all his children, not just his son Austin, were entitled to a quality, classical education. Education, honesty and hard work were his most important guiding principles. He saw education as the great liberating power in one's life. Naturally, as the son of Amherst Academy's founder, Edward Dickinson had both a personal and professional stake in seeing that his children had well-developed intellects. He also served as treasurer of nearby Amherst College from 1835 to 1837 and for another, lengthier term later in life. The academy and the college were closely linked, with faculty often moving between the two and a consistent curriculum. Therefore, the curricular standards at both institutions were as stringent and forward-looking as any in America.

In keeping with her father's wishes, Emily Dickinson attended Amherst Academy from 1840 to 1847. By every account, she was an excellent student. The list of subjects she studied there seems thoroughly modern and ordinary at first glance. English and classical literature, Latin, botany, geology, history, math and mental philosophy were the staples of the curriculum. However, the approach to the teaching of these subjects was different in the mid-nineteenth century. Every academic subject was placed within the context of the Christian religion. Even the rapidly expanding schools of thought in the natural sciences were seen only as proofs of the grandeur and sophistication of Creation.

The religious education at both Amherst Academy and College was held up by two essential pillars. First, the facts of the world each, in some way, provided evidence of divine influence. Around this time, the "watchmaker argument" for the existence of a higher power was very much in vogue. The argument stated that if one found a watch on the ground, one would conclude that some intelligent person had constructed the watch. Its complexity could not have happened by chance. The natural world, on the other hand, at first presents no such obvious level of complexity. However, the tools of science provide a way to peel back the superficial layers of the natural world and reveal a hidden complexity and order. Bodily organs, chemical reactions, seasonal phenomenon and all the other aspects of nature could be shown to be complex and purposeful, therefore arguing in favor of an intelligent creator. Scientific discoveries served only to add more proof of a creator working behind the scenes, bringing order to disorder. Dickinson internalized this perspective, but was less ready than her peers were to embrace a full conversion to the faith.

Dickinson continued to make friends at Amherst – there's no evidence that she was shy or withdrawn. Instead, she was part of an intimate circle of friends that she called "The Five." They included herself, Abiah Root, Abby Wood, Harriet Merrill and Sarah Tracy. Even after her academy days were over, Dickinson kept in close contact with several of her friends from youth. Her letters to these friends offer revealing insights to her personality, hopes and dreams. They reveal an intelligent but slightly rebellious young woman, interested in the revivals and conversions going on all around her but still stubbornly resistant to putting herself in the center of such public displays.

In her early teen years, Dickinson was frequently ill. She had serious bouts with the flu and missed many days at school, but given the time, this was not unusual. At one point, she missed almost an entire term at Amherst Academy. Dickinson's sickliness probably intensified her morbid fascination with and fear of death. As in childhood, she witnessed death firsthand as a teenager, as well.

In 1844, Dickinson's second cousin, Sophia Holland, passed away from a typhus infection. Once more, she came face to face with the horrible reality of death, and the experience was nearly too overpowering for her. She became ill herself, but her family was not sure how much of the illness was physical and how much was spiritual. At any rate, it was decided that young Emily should take a leave from school and spend time with family in Boston. About the same time, important changes were taken place back at Amherst College

Edward Hitchcock took over as college president in 1845. He was a powerful, influential figure who exemplified the idea that science was an extension and proof of religious truth. He strengthened the math and science curriculum, bringing the latest theories and research findings to the faculty. Thanks to his contributions, Emily Dickinson and her peers became as well versed in the scientific thought of the day as perhaps anybody in the country, outside of university faculty. Regardless, the basic idea remained that all science served a higher power and truth. Language was also an essential component of faith. In the mid-nineteenth century, many people believed that words were imbued with a kind of divine power. Naming things, as Adam in the Garden of Eden did, was a sacred act. The influence of Daniel Webster, the compiler of America's first dictionary, is clear in this. Webster fully believed that language was divine gift and the greatest distinguisher between humankind and the animal kingdom.

Dickinson absorbed the scientific teachings much more so than the religious teachings. At the same time, she learned several language and studied classical music. Curiously, she didn't learn to read a clock until she was 15. A modern reader might wonder whether Dickinson's young confusion about time might have shaped her personality in some way. As for literature, her tastes were broad but essentially in step with the times. She enjoyed the work of William Blake, Robert and Elizabeth Barrett Browning, and Charles Dickens. American literature was represented in the form of Ralph Waldo Emerson. The novels of Charles Dickens apparently held a special position for Dickinson, as she sometimes references characters and events from the novels in her letters.

Throughout her life, Dickinson had a conflicted relationship with her faith. She never publicly converted, which marked her as an outsider within the community. In letters to friends, she discussed her struggle to understand the meaning of religious faith. In 1847, there was yet another revival in Amherst, and Dickinson did not join in with the professions of devotion. She held back, apparently fearing that conversion would mean giving up her intellectual independence. This struggle to find her place in a deeply religious world found expression in many of her poems. That same year, she traveled once more to Boston to recuperate from yet another illness. In the fall of 1847, she returned west to begin her collegiate career at Mount Holyoke Female Seminary. While it perhaps seems strange that she attended a seminary in light of her religious doubts, it's important to remember that all education was fundamentally religious. Therefore, a "seminary" was not exactly distinct from any other higher learning establishment.

Well educated and fond of sermons disguised as lectures, Mary Lyon was the founder and superintendent of Mount Holyoke. Dickinson appreciated the educational rigor of the school, however, she wasn't seriously challenged – Amherst Academy had provided her with an exceptional foundation in most disciplines. Like Amherst, Mount Holyoke's instruction was grounded in religion. Dickinson had the good fortune of sharing a room with a cousin from Monson, Emily Lavinia Norcross. Despite these positive aspects, Dickinson was terribly homesick. Together with her parents, she decided that Mount Holyoke had nothing to offer that she didn't already have. In early 1848, Emily returned home to Amherst, where she remained for the rest of her life.

One of the last notable revivals came to Amherst in 1850. Dickinson wrote about the event, and it's clear that she had given up on the idea of making a public profession of faith. She realized that she was simply different from many of her friends and neighbors. Biographers believe that the three-year span from 1847 to 1850 is the period during which Dickinson began writing poetry.

Chapter 3: Early Career

The 1850s were a pivotal and transformative period in the life of Emily Dickinson. She went from being the studious academic to being the young woman with an uncertain role in life. She continued to have an active social life, attending parties and keeping in contact with many childhood friends. Most of these friends married and left town with their business-minded husbands. For Dickinson, suitors came and went, but she remained unmarried. At some point in her young adulthood, she made the conscious decision that she would forever remain in her father's home. However, the popular idea of a reclusive, friendless matron simply paints the wrong picture. In fact, Dickinson's eventual seclusion from the currents of the outside world was likely a deliberate choice that enabled her to devote as much time and energy as possible to the craft of writing.

Dickinson formed intense bonds with her closest friends, but her strongest, most intimate relationships were with her brother Austin and sister Lavinia ("Vinnie"). In some of her letters to Austin, she expressed almost a kind of jealously that he was so at liberty to go out and explore the wider world. Vinnie was more playful and flirtatious than her sister, but she too never married. Neither of Dickinson's siblings were quite her equal in terms of intellect and creativity.

More on Dickenson's intellectual level was Susan Gilbert, her future sister-in-law. Gilbert was only 9 days younger than Dickinson was. It's not clear how much Gilbert reciprocated the admiration of young Emily Dickinson. Some historians have wondered whether there was something more to their relationship, but none of the evidence suggests they were anything other than close friends. On Dickinson's side, she was perhaps uncomfortably close – her letters sometimes reveal possessiveness and rivalry with Austin for the affection of Susan. The pair became engaged around Thanksgiving 1853. At first, they considered a move to Michigan. There was potential for lucrative work in the interior, and Susan shared her husband's practical mind. Dickinson, however, was deeply hurt at the thought of losing both Austin and Susan. The family patriarch, Edward Dickinson, kept his son and daughter-in-law in Amherst by offering to build a house for them, to which they agreed. The new, spacious home was across the way from the Dickinson homestead; Austin aptly named the home "the Evergreens."

Even as an adult, Dickinson continued to look up to her powerful but distant father. However, in many ways she was more like her grandfather than her father. She had the intellect and passion of a dreamer, as well as a wide streak of independence. Edward approached life in a more workmanlike manner. He acted properly in everything and placed importance on earthly rewards and achievement. His Bible readings were an obligation that seemed to bring no joy or transcendence. Whereas Samuel Fowler Dickinson went bankrupt and lost the family home in pursuit of his ambition, Edward Dickinson steadily accumulated wealth and respectability. In 1855, he was even able to buy back the old homestead. The family moved back to the Brick House on Main Street, but all was not well. Dickinson's mother fell into mysterious illness that lasted until the early 1860s. The house evoked deep, horrid and unspeakable feelings in her that no one understood. Emily and her sister were constantly occupied in making sure their mother was cared for.

In nineteenth century Amherst, young Emily Dickinson had only two viable pathways set out before her. Ironically, her father, who was such a champion of liberal education for women, did not believe that women's roles in civic life should be expanded. Dickinson could marry, have children and most likely leave the place of her birth. She would only rarely see her family again, if at all. Her job from that point on would be to raise her offspring and keep house. The other alternative was to remain unmarried, a "spinster." Both of these options felt limiting, but Dickinson realized that marriage would mean a complete sacrifice of her own hopes and ambitions. So, just as she avoided a public conversion and the giving over of herself that act would require, so too did she turn away one suitor after another. Some of their names have remained: Ben Newton, George Gould, Henry Vaughn Emmons and John Graves would all try and fail to win Dickinson's affections. Of these, Graves would remain a lifelong friend and confidante. They would each, in time, find more sociable and but probably less interesting counterparts with which to spend their time.

Dickinson settled only gradually into her role in her father's house. Vinnie explained once that her sister was "the thinker." For her part, Vinnie became the manager of the house, owing to her mother's frequent illnesses and moodiness. This arrangement likely gave Emily more time to herself. In her cherished solitude, she began to compose some of her first poetry. Biographers have made admirable efforts to reconstruct a "timeline" of her poetic production. Most agree that Dickinson didn't transition from hobbyist to "full time" poet until around 1858. Sometimes, she enclosed a poem in a letter, which greatly helped in terms of dating the work. Prior to 1858, no year has more than one poem attached to it; after 1858, the numbers go up rapidly. Valentine's Day seems to have had a special attraction for Dickinson. Many of her early letters and poems are, in fact, valentines. This girlish fascination for a sweetheart's holiday reveals much about Dickinson's thinking. She was a romantic, but something always prevented her from taking the full plunge into romance. Possibly the same fear that held her back from public conversion also kept her from committing herself to marriage. The internal struggle between seeking inclusion and approval and needing solitude and independence would play itself out in many of her poems. Her intense and sometime volatile relationships with close friends and family also reveal something of this inner struggle, which as a young adult had yet to be settled. In the meantime, Dickinson privately began experimenting with turning her deepest feelings into a cryptic, mysterious kind of art.

No one can know for certain when Dickinson composed her first lines of poetry. The artfulness and wordplay for which Dickinson's poetry is so well known was equally on display in her letters, although in a different sense. While her letters were always vibrant, colorful and precisely crafted, by the mid-1850s, she had begun an even more self-conscious and deliberate effort to inject literary qualities into her writing. She used metaphors that were highly familiar to her friends and family, most of them borrowed from the Bible and popular sermons of the day. Religion infused life so strongly in the middle part of the 19th century that it was an almost inescapable influence. One of the most pervasive metaphors in the Trinitarian community of Amherst was the story of Jacob's wrestling with God on Mount Peniel. For Dickinson, then, poetry became a way to "wrestle" with the meaning of life, and, maybe more importantly, death.

As a young adult, Dickinson held onto her fascination with and fear of death. For her, the death of the body was not the only kind of death that haunted her. She also feared separation. Friends who moved far away became dead to her, especially when their letters stopped arriving with regularity. In the same sense, marriage symbolized a turning point in life that was similar to death. Dickinson displayed a neurotic fear of losing people. When she wrote to distant friends, she spent more energy describing her own pain and suffering caused by their absence than she did inquiring about her friend's wellbeing. Her choice to remain unmarried probably intensified her preoccupation with mortality. As a mother, she might have given more of her thought and energy to creating new life and raising a family. Choosing instead to remain a single woman, Dickinson's powerful creative impulse had to find an entirely different outlet.

In the context of struggling with death, Dickinson also drew upon imagery and metaphors from the Book of Revelations. Sickness and death became apocalyptic signs. An epidemic of scarlet fever in 1858 seemed like the end of things. In response, she secretly rejected the idea of a benevolent, fatherly God. Instead, she saw the unchecked power and unfeeling nature of God's work in the world and came to fear him. Doubts about life after death suffused her poetry and occupied her thought. Just as Jacob had wrestled God in the Old Testament, so too did Dickinson wrestle with God in Amherst. Her poetry became a way to test and define the nature of Divinity. Poetry was a private conversion for Dickinson, in contrast to the public conversion that she resisted.

Dickinson struggled with her identity in the several years following her return from Mount Holyoke. Between friends marrying and moving away, acquaintances dying from tuberculosis and fevers, change and instability seemed to be the norm. Life could be snatched away forever at a moment's notice. However, Dickinson eventually carved out an identity and vocation of her own, but she only hinted at this newfound "self" in her letters. The influence of her new sister-in-law Sue also had a restorative effect. The pair would collaborate on poetry and art, considering the merits or shortcomings of new authors and painters. Though she sent poems enclosed in letters to countless people, Emily sent more to Sue than anyone else.

#   #   #

In constructing her new identity, Dickinson made the acquaintance of several men in the still-fledgling literary industry. These included Thomas Wentworth Higginson, Samuel Bowels and Josiah Holland. She explained to Higginson that she intends her work to be universal rather than personal. She sent him four poems enclosed in a letter for him to critique. Of the few individuals who had to privilege of seeing her work, Higginson was one of the only ones who recognized the spark of brilliance within the difficult words and strange punctuation habits.

Dickinson's earliest poetry showed many repeating themes and ideas. The impression the poet left is one of meekness, humility and smallness. Many of the poems were forgivably juvenile and sentimental. However, a tinge of darkness and doubt had already crept into some of the work. Dickinson had a pessimistic outlook on human fate, even more so than most of her contemporaries, who witnessed just as much random disease and death as she did. She saw barrenness and uncertainty in human institutions. This uncertainty would inform all of her later work.

Chapter 4: Career, Works and Seclusion

As the 1850s gave way to the 1860s, Emily Dickinson gave more and more of her time to seclusion and the development of her craft. Her social life diminished gradually. Only a few of those closes to her even noticed her absences. Her sister Lavinia, for one, remarked that Dickinson was devoting more time to herself, but she did not see it as a problem. On some level, Lavinia understood particularly well what her sister needed to be happy, and a key factor was peace, quiet and alone time. Until at least the early 1860s, though, Dickinson did maintain a limited social life, albeit conducted entirely on her own terms.

Having Austin and Susan as next-door neighbors was one compelling reason for Dickinson to leave her room and venture outside. Even more compelling was the extraordinary guests that Susan invited to the Evergreens. These guests included some of the greatest luminaries of the day: Ralph Waldo Emerson, Henry Ward Beecher, Harriet Beecher Stowe, and Frederick Law Olmsted were just a few of the more familiar names. From about 1858 to 1861, Dickinson was a frequent visitor, soaking up new ideas and finding inspiration for new poems. Emily and her sister-in-law were kindred spirits from an intellectual perspective, but socially they were poles apart. Susan enjoyed festivities and attention. She was outspoken and always interested in the newest ideas and innovations. Austin and Susan's household was a cultural destination for everyone passing through Amherst. In time, Dickinson went next door less and less often, primarily because of her increasing dedication to her work and deliberate withdrawal from the noise and energy of ordinary people.

As Dickinson began to master her creative powers, she sent dozens of poems across the street to Sue. Some believe the pair maintained an informal "poetry workshop." Sue recognized the talents of her sister-in-law, but wasn't able to return the intensity of her passion. The almost pathetic strain of Dickinson's juvenile letters returned in her correspondence with Sue. In some instances, she placed Sue on a pedestal, allowing herself or the speaker of her poem to diminish almost to non-existence. Other times, anger flashed out, but never in a direct way. Later in life, the few people who interacted with Emily would remark that she had a haughty, off-putting demeanor.

As the relationship with Sue became more intimate by degrees, Dickinson seems to have grown cool toward Austin. For whatever reason, the tight bond of kinship was loosened. Some have speculated that Dickinson felt that Austin did not fully appreciate his brilliant, cultured partner. Like his father, he had distinct and conventional ideas as to the role of women in the household. He had no respect for the literary ambitions or reclusive tendencies of his artful sister. As for his wife, he envisioned her as the "Angel in the House" of the contemporary poet Coventry Patmore. It was a sickly sweet, but entirely normal view of women and matrimony at the time.

Dickinson herself traveled outside her small hometown on several occasions, although the trips were necessarily brief. She spent several days in nearby Springfield visiting the Hollands, close family friends. On another journey, she went south into Connecticut to visit her friend Eliza Coleman Dudley. There were also several trips to Boston, and even a lengthy excursion to the nation's capital when her father was in the Senate. Ultimately, it's not accurate to say that Dickinson *never* left Amherst, rather that she did so only rarely and purposively. Of course, the same was true for much of America's rural population in the 19th century. Travel for travel's sake and "vacations" had not actually entered anyone's vocabulary. The simple work of survival still demanded a great deal of attention.

Lavinia Norcross, a maternal aunt who was never in excellent health, died from tuberculosis in 1860. It was a shocking event for both of the Dickinson nieces. Vinnie had traveled hurriedly to attend her aunt's illness, but she was too late to be useful. Norcross was just shy of 50 years old, and she left behind two daughters: Louisa and Francis. Emily sent warm condolences to her young cousins, and they all became fast friends. Eventually, the Norcross girls received many of Dickinson's most personal and heartfelt letters, and not a few poems. She took on an almost motherly role to Louisa and Francis, even though many miles separated them. The Norcross cousins witnessed a side of Dickinson that few others saw, including even Susan. When they visited Amherst, she treated them to readings of her poetry and songs. She was not half so playful with any of her other close friends. Like Dickinson, Francis and Louisa also shunned orthodox religion, eventually joining the same liberal church as Ralph Waldo Emerson.

In 1861, Dickinson first began experiencing one of the greatest crises of her life. Her eyesight, which had never been excellent, began to seriously degrade. Poor eyesight was common among the Dickinsons. Austin possibly had the worst eyesight of any of the siblings, but for Emily, losing her sight would have been a nightmarish outcome. From 1861 through 1865, ironically coinciding with the American Civil War, Dickinson had every reason to believe that she was steadily going blind. Bright light was unbearable to her, and she was urged not to spend much time reading or writing. Her handwriting during this time went from bad to almost illegible. In 1862, fearing that her work of the last several years might be lost or misplaced, she wrote or transcribed hundreds of poems – 366 to be exact.

Dickinson did not go blind, but she also did not experience improvement in her condition. She went to Cambridge several times in 1864 and 1865 to see a vision specialist. The efforts were successful, as most of her vision was eventually restored. After returning from her last visit to the specialist in October 1865, Dickinson was determined to never leave home again, if possible. Instead, she wished to concentrate even more intensely on her work – her poetry, in other words. She had escaped a disabling blindness, and she knew that death and disease might strike her down at any time. She saw her friends less and less, often making up excuses to apologize for her absence. Her sister explained that Emily's seclusion came on little by little. Her removal from society, therefore, cannot be traced to any momentous turning point or event.

In 1862, while in the depths of her eye disease, Dickinson sent a letter to the abolitionist Thomas Wentworth Higginson. He had just published an article in the *Atlantic Monthly* concerning young writers, and Dickinson was intrigued. She enclosed four poems in her letter and shyly asked for a critique. Of the few who glimpsed her poetry during her life, many were turned away be its cryptic nature and highly unusual styling, but not Higginson. It was the first step in a productive friendship that would last the rest of Dickinson's life. After her death, he was instrumental in preserving Dickinson's lifetime of work and ensuring that it eventually saw the light of day. Higginson was happy to offer his suggestions, but he sensed that he was out of his depth. The poetry he received was more unusual and strangely compelling than any he had ever read. This was one of the first times that Dickinson had sought advice regarding her art. It was a profound declaration that she intended to pursue a writing life for the rest of her days.

When Higginson visited the Dickinson's Brick House many years later, he encountered a shy, child-like, but brilliantly perceptive woman. He described the pitter-patter of her steps approaching the door and her initial reluctance to talk. Once she became comfortable in his presence, she talked at length on numerous subjects. Nevertheless, he found her to be an overwhelming, nerve-wracking powerhouse of a women and was glad to say that could not see her more often.

#   #   #

It's impossible to discuss Dickinson's adult life without considering the impact of the American Civil War. However, as with most of the details of her life, evidence of the war's effect on her is scarce and often indirect. Many biographers and critics have concluded that being far away from the fighting, Dickinson had no relationship with the national struggle. That would be an incorrect assumption, though, because poems and correspondences from the time reveal that she did indeed think long and hard about the meaning of the Civil War. For one thing, the young men of Massachusetts were called to fight in large numbers. This effectively brought the battle home, as sons and brothers marched south toward an uncertain fate.

War made death even more generalized and random than it otherwise was. At the same time, Dickinson invested strongly in the capacity for meaningful, heroic acts in the face of national tragedy. Like Whitman, she saw the almost majestic importance of the war. She believed in the values of freedom, self-determination and human equality, even if she didn't announce it from the rooftops. When her eye disease did not prevent her from writing, Dickinson produced some of her most intense and powerful work during the Civil War. Her tone and voice matured and lost all vestiges of the child-like juvenilia of the 1850s. Sue and her cousins witnessed the change and recognized the full flowering of Dickinson's power. The war years provided a powerful impetus to redefine and reshape the idea of American-ness. Dickinson embarked on the project with fervor.

In the years leading up to the conflict, Edward Dickinson was on the side of reconciliation. He was a leading figure in the Constitutional Unionist Party, which denounced the heated rhetoric coming from the North and South. His daughter seems to have been ambivalent at first, sometimes admiring her father's patriotism and other times ironically mocking the stuffiness of politicians. Edward was even asked to run on the party's ticket for president, but he quickly declined. At any rate, Lincoln won the office outright, and the Constitutional Unionists were demoralized and broken. After hostilities began, the Republican Party requested Edward to join the ticket for lieutenant governor. He again declined, writing a public letter that denounced the emancipation of the slaves. In response, he was ridiculed and disgraced. It was no doubt a troubling experience for Emily, seeing her father brought down by the viciousness of political attacks. Nevertheless, Edward still supported the Union efforts in practical, if not philosophical ways. He sent passionate letters to Union leaders, warning that the result of the war would be a wasted nation and the end of a great experiment in democracy. His associates never comprehended quite where he stood, at some moments arguing for state's rights and in another praising the efforts of Lincoln to reconstitute the nation. For a man so wedded to civil society, the war must have been extremely difficult for his mental health and wellbeing.

Emily Dickinson's relationship with the Civil War was even more difficult to define than her father's was. Of course, Amherst was hundreds to thousands of miles away from actual battlefields. The carnage that Whitman and other war journalists witnessed up close was only born north in the form of occasional reports that never captured the full intensity of the combat. There were few pictures, and numerical reports of casualties have always had an abstraction to them that effectively distance the mind from actual horror. Dickinson declined the typical duty of making bandages and blankets for the soldiers. In her writing, she remarks that Sue and Vinnie are more ardent in their patriotic support of the young men gone to war. Instead, Dickinson seemed more concerned with the personal, interior war that each soldier, and to some extent, each citizen had to fight within their own heart. She sympathized deeply when friends and neighbors lost sons in the fighting. Above all, the war provided an epically absurd terror from which to draw scraps of meaning and inspiration. This is not to say that Dickinson "prettified" the Civil Way; she distilled its essence into her art in her own particular way.

The Civil War even provided an outlet for the publication of a small number of Dickinson's poems. Three appeared in the modest Brooklyn paper *Drum Beat* in 1864, a periodical that had the purpose of generating funds for Union soldiers' medical care. A year later, another poem, "Success is Counted Sweetest," was published in the *Brooklyn Daily Union*. These two instances are among the rare occasions when Dickinson allowed her work to reach an audience outside of her immediate family and trusted friends. In other cases of publication, poetry was submitted without her consent. In nearby Springfield, a fundraising fair was held in 1864. Austin was asked to provide some artwork for an exhibit, be he declined. Likewise, Emily declined to provide any poetry to the fair's newsletter. It is not clear what motivated Dickinson to give her work to one publication but not to another. It is clear that in the majority of cases, she refused any requests to supply writing of any kind.

#   #   #

Dickinson's poetry was thoroughly modern, even post-modern, and, therefore, decades ahead of its time. Dozens of her poems are, in fact, "poems about poems," or about creating art or being an artist. The level of self-consciousness on display is evidence that Dickinson saw poetry as a vocation rather than just a hobby. It was a way for her to approach problems that had haunted her since she was old enough to think deeply about the world. Because the problems she approached were themselves difficult, having to do with existence and purpose, the structure and verbiage of the poems are likewise difficult. On first glance, she seems to have put little forethought into the structure and meter of her poetry. Closer inspection, though, reveals a carefully crafted, expert level of construction in most of Dickinson's work. They often follow the cadences of hymns, religious songs with which she would have been familiar.

Dickinson's poetry might be most famous for its frequent use of the dash. Her handwritten poems reveal dashes of different sizes and shapes, so it's possible that she had an entire system in her mind. The dashers serve to break up the poems, both visually and thematically, opening them up to many interpretations. Dashes force the reader or speaker to pause for breath and consider the importance of the preceding lines. Even today, readers can strongly disagree over the intent behind certain lines. Few poets from the 19th century still inspire so much questioning and debate. In hindsight, the structural regularity of Dickinson's poetry becomes clear. She wrote largely in the metrical style of hymns, with lines of 8 and 6 syllables in length. Early editorial changes often obscured this regularity. However, she used the hymn structure as only a starting point from which to depart along experimental pathways.

Beyond structural elements, such as dashes and off-rhymes, Dickinson's poetry exhibited a kind of voice that has rarely, if ever, been reproduced. The speaker in the poems seems to address the reader directly, almost as if interviewing the reader. Typically, poetry presents itself as something "overheard" – something outside of the reader's existence, not necessarily addressing the reader at all. Dickinson took a different approach. The "personability" of her poetic voice was not just an accident. She worked hard to create this sensation. This relationship between voice and reader is one more factor that has helped Dickinson's work remain as popular and vibrant as it has. With the exception of some word choices, her best poetry reads as if it might have been written yesterday.

Modern readers might expect that Dickinson would have used her poetry to speak to great events of the time, or stand on a soapbox for women's rights as some of her contemporaries did. Nothing could be further from the truth. Instead, Dickinson shied away from overt politics and social issues. She hinted at these ideas but never communicated many clear opinions on world events or the plight of women. In a few letters, she even expressed some disdain for the most outspoken women's rights activists. Dickinson saw endless shades of grey in the world, whereas activists and those fighting for causes saw only black and white. She believed that her contribution to making the world better should come in the form of art, not politicking. Therefore, in none of her writing was there any feeling of bitterness at her fate – the fate of being born a woman. She did not ignore the role her gender played in shaping her life, but neither did she exploit it for short-lived sympathy or pleading.

The themes and issues in Dickinson's poetry remained constant throughout her adult life. While her younger years did include some sentimental work, by the 1860s she was giving all of her energy to her most difficult and painful questions. Specifically, she struggled to understand the meaning of life in a world where pain and death were so commonplace. Many of her poems evoke a sense of being wounded or fearful. In other poems, the tone is ecstatic, even erotic, which many readers and critics find intriguing in light of the author's quiet, chaste lifestyle. Even death could create a sensation not unlike sexual attraction, especially when death is personified as a kind gentleman. Dickinson frequently created situations where the speaker faces a profound decision or turning point. Change, confrontation, fate and mystery are dominant themes that infuse the majority of the poems.

Harkening back to her days as a student at Amherst Academy and Mount Holyoke, many of Dickinson's poems have a peculiar fixation on mathematics, geometry, science and astronomy. Some poems read almost like math problems translated into a strange kind of language. Dickinson was also fascinated with time, in particular the idea of "noon." Even the word noon is fascinating – it reads the same forwards and backward. It's also two "nos" facing each other. Dickinson enjoyed subtle wordplay, experimenting with not only meanings but sounds and shapes, too. Modern readers sometimes complain that the poetry is not easy to read aloud. This has led critics to state that it was never meant to be read aloud. The historical record contradicts this, though. There is ample evidence that Dickinson read her poetry to her cousins and Sue, and probably many more besides. Lou Norcross remembers that her cousin had a unique and bewitching way of reciting the verses that only intensified the various shades of meaning and ambiguity.

In spite of positive feedback from the likes of Higginson, Samuel Bowles and others, Dickinson rarely sought to have her work published, even at the height of her production. Her reluctance to publish is ironic, given the nature of her poetry, which clearly addresses the reader in a strong, personable voice. Her sister Vinnie never comprehended just how much her quiet, solitary sister was writing while alone in her chamber. Instead of publication for the masses, Dickinson created a kind of self-publication. Between 1858 and 1864, she bound hundreds of her poems in delicate, finely crafted booklets called "fascicles." Bound together with string and numbering forty in all, these books in miniature were not discovered until after her death. Scholars have debated at length as to whether the fascicles have an organizing principle behind them. Some argue that specific thematic concerns prevail in each of the fascicles, while others claim that the arrangement is just chronological. As with all aspects of understanding Dickinson and her work, the issue of her fascicles is one of heated debate. Her construction of fascicles also made it difficult to establish a date on many of the poems, so biographers have had to make educated guesses.

Scores of Dickinson's poems fall into the category of love or erotic poetry. This has naturally led to speculation that she had one or possibly several lovers during her adult life. Susan Gilbert is frequently mentioned as a possible romantic partner, but the evidence just doesn't add up. Nor do any men cross her path often enough to constitute a real, physical relationship, with the exception of one person near the end of her life. There is some strong evidence of what might be called flirtation between Reverend Charles Wadsworth and Dickinson, but his side of the correspondence is lost. Ultimately, the love poetry simply has to be read in the context of imagination. The poem's speaker is a projection, not an autobiographical witness of the poet's life. Some of the love poetry evokes the image of "the wife," quietly attending to the needs of those around her. The metaphor is taken to its highest level with the use of images of Christ and the Crucifixion. All things considered, readers must remember that Dickinson led a quiet life, despite the activity of her imagination.

Despite the well-documented problems with her vision, the first half of the 1860s proved to be the most productive years of Dickinson's poetic career. At times, she likely drafted several poems in a single day. There are several possible explanations to account for this high creative output. First, mother and father were in relatively good health. Mother was recovering from the shock of moving back into the Brick House. Father was always occupied with business. Emily had the run of the house, with hours each day to herself. By the late 1850s, she had most likely resolved that she would never marry, which may have freed her heart and spirit to concentrate entirely on her art.

Chapter 5: Later Life and Death

By the late 1860s, Emily Dickinson's rate of poetry writing had slowed down considerably. Even her production of letters had decreased. Still not quite 40 years old, she seemingly had moved beyond her prime years of creativity. She finished a few dozen pieces each year, but she no longer made any of the cleverly constructed fascicles. Between 1866 and 1871 Dickinson composed only about 70 poems, fewer than she composed during even a single year in the earlier part of the decade. There's no single reason why her productivity decreased. Numerous factors worked together to turn Dickinson's attention elsewhere, but pure exhaustion might have been the most obvious culprit.

In the winter of 1866, Dickinson's beloved dog, Carlos, died. He had been her companion since 1850. In letters to Higginson, it's clear that the loss affected her deeply. Around the same time, the Dickinsons' household help, Margaret O'Bryan, was married and left Amherst. Vinnie and Emily, therefore, had to absorb more of the housework. The sisters enjoyed their surplus of time together, baking bread and cakes and cleaning up after dinners. The extra work also meant less time for solitude and writing. Emily took the changes in stride. She appreciated the opportunity to work with her hands, helping the house to run smoothly despite the lack of domestic help. The relatively few poems that she does write during this period have a different tone to them – less combative, more reserved, slightly less cryptic – but they retained Dickinson's unique mode of expression.

Edward Dickinson did well for himself in the post-war years. His activities in the church declined, but he spent more time tending to his business interests. With a net worth approaching $50,000, he wielded his influence one more time when he brought the Massachusetts Agricultural College to Amherst. Today, the campus is known as the University of Massachusetts at Amherst. As for his relationship with his poet daughter, it became as icy and remote as ever. Even Austin withdrew from his sister, and he and Sue made deliberate efforts to safeguard their own children against the solitary, introspective life of a poet.

Although she saw fewer and fewer visitors, Emily Dickinson seems to have let go of some of her neuroticism regarding affection and separation. Instead, she recognized that the yearning for another is like a spell that's broken when the other is nearby. She learned that individuals never quite match her idealized fantasies. In turn, her poetry from the 1870s is again more sedate, reflective and often preoccupied with the concept of memory. Dickinson did not necessarily dwell on her own memories, but rather the collective memory of people. There was also a tinge of regret when she recalled her younger years. However, no one knows what the source of such regret might have been, or why she withdrew from people even more as she entered her forties.

At an unspecified point, Dickinson began wearing nothing but white housedresses. They were simple, loose and inelegant. Some have suggested that she wore white as a symbol of her commitment to an "order" of her own creation. Her only surviving article of clothing, a white dress with cuffs and a round collar, dates to around 1870. Joseph Lyman wrote an absurdly fantastic article about a meeting with Dickinson where he emphasizes her whiteness and smallness. Higginson noticed, as well. When he met the poet for the first time in 1870, he described her as childlike but also exhausting. Writing to his wife, he remarked that he was glad not to live near her.

When old friends passed through town, Dickinson frequently refused to meet them. Abby Wood remarked that her old friend was treated like a high priestess. She didn't appreciate the cold reception of her former playmate, and told her so. In some cases, Dickinson would speak with a guest from the other side of a door, literally not wanting to be "seen." The admittedly odd behavior earned her a mix of awe and scorn within the community, though it's unlikely that Emily would have noticed either way.

Dickinson's writing picked up once more in the 1870s, but it never returned to the breakneck pace set in earlier years. Nor did she go to much trouble in terms of organizing the work. She would sometimes go as far as making a clean copy of a particular poem, but more often the poems remained as they were written – scribbled on an envelope, pamphlet, or whatever was handy. After her death, the organization of her notes and papers proved to be a momentous task.

By 1873, Edward Dickinson had become feeble. His children watched cautiously as his health failed. He had already stepped down from his post as Amherst College treasurer. Still, he continued to invest his time in local and state politics, regardless of his diminished strength. This accounts for why he was in Boston when a severe stroke ended his life on June 16, 1874. Curiously, he never composed a will, despite being a lawyer and having a firm grasp of financial matters. As such, his estate fell under the management of Austin, who lorded over Vinnie and Emily next door. Even Austin's children adopt a condescending attitude toward their aunts.

Exactly one year after Edward's death, his widow suffered a profound stroke. Half of her body was paralyzed, and her memory was severely impaired. This once more placed a burden on the Dickinson siblings, and Emily had even less time to give to her craft. The Dickinson matriarch lingered on until November 1882.

In 1877, Dickinson became close with Judge Otis Phillips Lord. It's possible that their relationship was slightly more than Platonic. Lord had recently lost his wife, while Dickinson was feeling overwhelmed by the coldness of Austin and the demands of her disabled mother. None of their letters have survived, which is often taken as evidence that they maintained a secret romance. Most people kept the poet's letters, owing to their charm and sophisticated language. Lord passed away in 1884.

As family and friends aged and passed on, Dickinson felt the world closing in around her. She made her sister the trustee of her worldly possessions, instructing her to burn everything upon her death. In 1884, she suffered a fainting spell and was bedridden for some time. A year later, she became so ill that Austin worried she would die at any moment. Bedridden, Dickinson produced no letters or poetry until the following spring, when she sent out her last few. She took her last breath on May 15, 1886, aged 55 years. Her physician identified kidney disease as the cause of her long illness.

Fortunately for the literary world, Vinnie disobeyed her sister's request to burn her papers. She also discovered the forty-some fascicles tucked away amongst stacks of paper and letters. Recognizing the literary merit of the long-hidden work, Vinnie set out to find an editor for her sister's papers. Higginson and Mabel Loomis Todd, Austin's mistress, took upon themselves the organizing of Dickinson's work for publication. The first posthumous volume was released in 1890, and two more quickly followed. The popular reception was overwhelmingly positive, though critics were uncertain what to make of the mysterious woman from Amherst. It's vital to note that Higginson and Todd, along with many subsequent editors, took great liberties with the verse. Dashes were removed, punctuation regularized, and difficult words replaced in order to make the poetry more palatable.

In 1955, Thomas H. Johnson produced the first truly scholarly publication of Emily Dickinson's poetry. In the three-volume set, he restored the punctuation to its original form for first time. He also did away with Higginson and Todd's arbitrary titles, choosing instead to number the poems chronologically. Johnson's work set in motion a great wave of Dickinson scholarship. Interest in and appreciation for Dickinson's immense contributions to literature grew beyond the walls of academia, and she became lauded as a fundamentally American voice every bit as important as Walt Whitman or Henry David Thoreau.

Chapter 6: Legacy

Historians and biographers attempt to piece together the preserved fragments of a life in an attempt to recreate a personality. When the person being studied is an artist, facts and events from his or her life often bring illumination to the art itself. In Emily Dickinson's case, the usual pattern has been reversed. So little remains of the mundane, tangible details of her lived existence that many have taken the approach of exploring her life through the lens of her poetry. This pursuit is doomed to failure, however. Myth has replaced reality. Many imagine that Dickinson was a hermit, perhaps even mentally ill, with a rare talent for writing poetry. The talent part is certainly true, but it's unfair to think she might have been mentally or emotionally unstable. Nevertheless, the image of the lonely, secluded poet has become a highly romantic image, both for Dickinson and for many poets to follow.

By the middle of the 20th century, Emily Dickinson had taken her place alongside Walt Whitman as twin icons of American literature. In 1955, her complete works were released, with all posthumous editorial changes removed. For the first time, readers could see Dickinson's work just as she intended, or nearly so. The characteristic punctuation, off rhymes and unexpected rhythms were on full display. Dickinson's reputation grew even more powerful in light of the new publication, and she became required reading for American literature students from public school up through higher education. She's one of only a few modern poets whose influence has extended beyond the walls of academia and penetrated the public's imagination.

Whereas Walt Whitman composed big, sweeping poetry that scanned the cities and frontiers in search of quintessential "America," Dickinson's poetry was more focused and personal, almost laser-like in the search for absolute meanings. Her concerns were with the inner life of the mind, life and death, and the meaning of existence in the face of unpredictable nature. Many have commented that her poems function like word puzzles begging to be solved. A century and a half later, those puzzles are still points of debate. Few poets have produced work that is so open to such a variety of interpretation.

In the 20th century, William Carlos Williams would identify Emily Dickinson as his "patron saint" of poetry. The Beat Generation of poets also looked to Dickinson as a source of inspiration. They admired her courage in rowing against the current of her time, producing work that was too revolutionary for her contemporaries to understand. Women writers, too, have found a kindred spirit in Dickinson. While she was never outspokenly a suffragist or campaigner for equal rights, her choices in life became small acts of defiance in themselves. By choosing to follow her own ambition rather than the expectations of society, Dickinson was a rebel and independent spirit. That rebelliousness has became as much a part of her legacy as her seclusion for the social world in later life.

Conclusion

Emily Dickinson's unique and enduring contributions to American literature cannot be overstated. Many literary authorities have placed Dickinson on the short list of all-time greatest poets in any language. Indeed, her poetry's unique capacity for communicating directly to readers across time and space has made Dickinson a celebrated poet of *the world*, not just America. While the life she lived was certainly humble and small, the impression she made on her closest friends was powerful. It's incredible to think that her nearly 2,000 individual poems might have been lost to history but for the foresight of her sister and close friend Thomas Wentworth Higginson.

Bibliography

Bauer, Dale and Philip Gould, eds. *The Cambridge Companion to Nineteenth-Century American Women's Writing*. New York: Cambridge UP, 2001.

"Emily Dickinson." (2009). Emily Dickinson Museum online.
http://www.emilydickinsonmuseum.org/node/18

"Emily Dickinson." (2013). Poetry Foundation.
http://www.poetryfoundation.org/bio/emily-dickinson

"Emily Dickinson." (2013). Poets.org.
http://www.poets.org/poet.php/prmPID/155

"Emily Dickinson." (2012). Wikipedia.
http://en.wikipedia.org/wiki/Emily_Dickinson

Freedman, Linda. *Emily Dickinson and the Religious Imagination*. New York: Cambridge UP, 2011.

Habegger, Alfred. *My Wars Are Laid Away in Books: The Life of Emily Dickinson*. New York: Random House, 2001.

Oberhaus, Dorothy Huff. "About Dickinson's 'Fascicles.'" *Modern American Poetry.* **http://www.english.illinois.edu/maps/poets/a_f/dickinson/fascicles.htm**

Wolff, Cynthia. *Emily Dickinson*. New York: Alfred A. Knopf, 1987.

Printed in Great Britain
by Amazon.co.uk, Ltd.,
Marston Gate.